Aristophanes

Lysistrata

Translated
by
Ian Johnston
Vancouver Island University
Nanaimo, British Columbia
Canada

Richer Resources Publications
Arlington, Virginia
USA

Aristophanes
Lysistrata

Richer Resources Publications
1926 N. Woodrow Street
Arlington, Virginia 22207
or via our web site at
www.RicherResourcesPublications.com

ISBN 978-0-9818162-3-4
Library of Congress Control Number 2008931604

Published by Richer Resources Publications
Arlington, Virginia
Printed in the United States of America

Aristophanes
Lysistrata

Aristophanes
Lysistrata

Translator's Note

In the text below the numbers in square brackets refer to the lines in the Greek text; the numbers without brackets refer to the lines in the translated text. In numbering the lines of the English text, the translator has normally counted a short indented line with the short line above it, so that two short lines count as one line.

In a number of places in *Lysistrata* there is some confusion over which speeches are assigned to which people. These moments occur, for the most part, in short conversational exchanges. Hence, there may be some differences between the speakers in this text and those in other translations.

The translator would like to acknowledge the valuable help provided by Alan H. Sommerstein's edition of *Lysistrata* (Aris & Phillips: 1990), particularly the commentary.

Historical Note

Aristophanes (c. 447 to c. 385) was the foremost writer of Old Comedy in Athens. His play *Lysistrata* was first produced in Athens in 411 BC. By this time Athens and Sparta had been at war for about twenty years.

Aristophanes
Lysistrata

Dramatis Personae

LYSISTRATA: a young Athenian wife
CALONICE: a mature married woman
MYRRHINE: a teenage wife
LAMPITO: a young country wife from Sparta
ISMENIA: a woman from Thebes
SCYTHIAN GIRL: one of Lysistrata's slaves
MAGISTRATE: an elderly Athenian official
CINESIAS: husband of Myrrhine
CHILD: infant son of Myrrhine and Cinesias
MANES: servant nurse of the Child
HERALD: A Spartan envoy
CHORUS OF OLD MEN
CHORUS OF OLD WOMEN
ATHENIAN AMBASSADOR
SPARTAN AMBASSADOR
WOMAN A: one of the wives following Lysistrata
WOMAN B: one of the wives following Lysistrata
WOMAN C: one of the wives following Lysistrata
ARMED GUARDS: police officials attending on the Magistrate
WOMEN: followers of Lysistrata
RECONCILIATION: a goddess of harmony and peace
ATHENIAN DELEGATES
SPARTAN DELEGATES
SLAVES AND ATTENDANTS.

[The action of the play takes place in a street in Athens, with the citadel on the Acropolis in the back, its doors facing the audience]

LYSISTRATA
    If they'd called a Bacchic celebration
    or some festival for Pan or Colias
    or for Genetyllis, you'd not be able
    to move around through all the kettle drums.
    But as it is, there are no women here.

[Calonice enters, coming to meet Lysistrata]

Ah, here's my neighbour—at least she's come.[1]
Hello, Calonice.

CALONICE

Hello, Lysistrata.
What's bothering you, child? Don't look so annoyed.
It doesn't suit you. Your eyes get wrinkled.

LYSISTRATA

My heart's on fire, Calonice—I'm so angry   10
at married women, at us, because,   [10]
although men say we're devious characters . . .

CALONICE [interrupting]
Because by god we are!

LYSISTRATA [continuing]
                        . . . when I call them all
to meet here to discuss some serious business,
they just stay in bed and don't show up.

CALONICE
Ah, my dear, they'll come. It's not so easy
for wives to get away. We've got to fuss
about our husbands, wake up the servants,
calm and wash the babies, then give them food . . .

LYSISTRATA
But there are other things they need to do—   20   [20]
more important issues.

CALONICE

My dear Lysistrata,
why have you asked the women to meet here?
What's going on? Is it something big?

LYSISTRATA

It's huge.

CALONICE
And hard as well?

---

[1] . . . at least she's come. Lysistrata is complaining that if the city had called a major festival all the women would be in the streets enjoying themselves. But none of them, it seems, has answered her invitation to a meeting (as we find out a few lines further on).

LYSISTRATA

        Yes, by god, really hard.

CALONICE

Then why aren't we all here?

LYSISTRATA

        I don't mean that!
If that were it, they'd all be charging here so fast.
No. It's something I've been playing with—
wrestling with for many sleepless nights.

CALONICE

If you've been working it like that, by now
it must have shrivelled up.

LYSISTRATA

        Yes, so shrivelled up   30
that the salvation of the whole of Greece   [30]
is now in women's hands.

CALONICE

        In women's hands?
Then it won't be long before we done for.

LYSISTRATA

It's up to us to run the state's affairs—
the Spartans would no longer be around.

CALONICE

If they weren't there, by god, not any more,
that would be good news.

LYSISTRATA

        And then if all Boeotians
were totally destroyed!

CALONICE

        Not all of them—
you'd have to save the eels.[1]

---

[1] ... *save the eels.* At the time *Lysistrata* was first produced, the Athenians and Spartans had been fighting for many years. The Boeotians were allies of the Spartans. Boeotia was famous for its eels, considered a luxury item in Athens.

7

LYSISTRATA
                              As for Athens,
I won't say anything as bad as that.   40
You can imagine what I'd say. But now,
if only all the women would come here
from Sparta and Boeotia, join up with us,   [40]
if we worked together, we'd save Greece.

CALONICE
But what sensible or splendid act
could women do? We sit around playing
with our cosmetics, wearing golden clothes,
posing in Cimmerian silks and slippers.

LYSISTRATA
Those are the very things which I assume
will save us—short dresses, perfumes, slippers,   50
make up, and clothing men can see through.

CALONICE
How's that going to work?

LYSISTRATA
                              No man living
will lift his spear against another man . . .   [50]

CALONICE *[interrupting]*
By the two goddesses, I must take my dress
and dye it yellow.[1]

LYSISTRATA *[continuing]*
                              . . . or pick up a shield . . .

CALONICE *[interrupting again]*
I'll have to wear my very best silk dress.

LYSISTRATA *[continuing]*
. . . or pull out his sword.

CALONICE
                              I need to get some shoes.

---

[1] . . . *dye it yellow.* The two goddesses are Demeter and her daughter Persephone. The
Athenian women frequently invoke them.

8

LYSISTRATA
O these women, they should be here by now!

CALONICE
Yes, by god! They should have sprouted wings
and come here hours ago.

LYSISTRATA
They're true Athenians,   60
you'll see—everything they should be doing
they postpone till later. But no one's come
from Salamis or those towns on the coast.

CALONICE [with an obscene gesture]
I know those women—they were up early
on their boats riding the mizzen mast.   [60]

LYSISTRATA
I'd have bet
those women from Acharnia would come
and get here first. But they've not shown up.

CALONICE
Well, Theogenes' wife will be here.
I saw her hoisting sail to come.¹ Hey, look!
Here's a group of women coming for you.   70
And there's another one, as well. Hello!
Hello there! Where they from?

[Various women start arriving from all directions]

LYSISTRATA
Those? From Anagyra.

CALONICE
My god, it seems we're kicking up a stink.²

[Enter Myrrhine]

MYRRHINE
Hey, Lysistrata, did we get here late?
What's the matter? Why are you so quiet?

¹ Theogenes: a well-known merchant and shipowner.

² ... a stink: Calonice is making an obscure joke on the name Anagyra, a political district
named after a bad-smelling plant.

9

LYSISTRATA

I'm not pleased with you, Myrrhine. You're late.   [70]
And this is serious business.

MYRRHINE

                        It was dark.
I had trouble tracking down my waist band.
If it's such a big deal, tell these women.

LYSISTRATA

No, let's wait a little, until the women   80
from Boeotia and from Sparta get here.

MYRRHINE

All right. That sounds like the best idea.
Hey, here comes Lampito.

[Lampito enters with some other Spartan women and with Ismenia, a woman from Thebes]

LYSISTRATA

                        Hello Lampito,
my dear friend from Sparta. How beautiful
you look, so sweet, such a fine complexion.   [80]
And your body looks so fit, strong enough
to choke a bull.

LAMPITO[1]

                        Yes, by the two gods,
I could pull that off.[2] I do exercise
and work out to keep my bum well toned.

CALONICE *[fondling Lampito's bosom]*
What an amazing pair of breasts you've got!   90

---

[1]LAMPITO: In Aristophanes' text, Lampito and other Spartans use a parody of a Spartan dialect, a style of speaking significantly different from (although related to) Athenian Greek. Translators have dealt with this in different ways, often by giving the Spartans a recognizable English dialect, for example, from the Southern States or Scotland. Here I have not tried to follow this trend, since such dialects as often as not are unfamiliar to many readers.

[2]*. . . the two gods*: Spartans commonly invoke the divine twins Castor and Pollux, brothers of Helen of Troy.

LAMPITO
O, you stroke me like I'm a sacrifice.⌉

LYSISTRATA *[looking at Ismenia]*
And this young woman—where's she from?   [90]

LAMPITO
By the twin gods, she's an ambassador—
she's from Boeotia.

MYRRHINE *[looking down Ismenia's elegant clothes]*
                    Of course, from Boeotia.
She's got a beautiful lowland region.

CALONICE *[peering down the dress to check Ismenia's pubic hair]* ⟵
Yes. By god, she keeps that territory
elegantly groomed.

LYSISTRATA
                    Who's the other girl?

LAMPITO
A noble girl, by the two gods, from Corinth.

CALONICE *[inspecting the girl's bosom and buttocks]*
A really noble girl, by Zeus—it's clear   ⌉
she's got good lines right here, back here as well.   100

LAMPITO
All right, who's the one who called the meeting
and brought this bunch of women here?

LYSISTRATA
                    I did.

LAMPITO
Then lay out what it is you want from us.

MYRRHINE
Come on, dear lady, tell us what's going on,
what's so important to you.

LYSISTRATA
                    In a minute.
Before I say it, I'm going to ask you
one small question . . .

⌐ body image   11

CALONICE
>Ask whatever you want.

LYSISTRATA
>Don't you miss the fathers of your children
>when they go off to war? I understand
>you all have husbands far away from home.

[100]

110

CALONICE
>My dear, it's five full months my man's been gone—
>off in Thrace taking care of Eucrates.

MYRRHINE
>And mine's been off in Pylos seven whole months.[1]

LAMPITO
>And mine—as soon as he gets home from war,
>he grabs his shield and buggers off again.

LYSISTRATA
>As for old flames and lovers—there're none left.
>And since Milesians went against us,
— >I've not seen a decent eight-inch dildo.
>Yes, it's just leather, but it helps us out.[2]
>So would you be willing, if I found a way,
>to work with me to make this fighting end?

[110]

120

MYRRHINE
>By the twin goddesses, yes. Even if
>in just one day I had to pawn this dress
>and drain my purse.

CALONICE
>Me too—they could slice me up
>like a flat fish, then use one half of me
>to get a peace.

LAMPITO
>I'd climb up to the top

[1] . . . *after Eucrates.* Thrace is a region to the north of Greece, a long way from Athens. Eucrates was an Athenian commander in the region. Pylos is a small area in the south Peloponnese which the Athenians had occupied for a number of years.

[2] . . . *went against us.* Miletus had rebelled against Athens in the previous year. That city was associated with sexuality and (in this case) the manufacture of sexual toys.

of Taygetus to get a glimpse of peace.[1]

LYSISTRATA
　　All right I'll tell you. No need to keep quiet
　　about my plan. Now, ladies, if we want　　　　　　　[120]
　　to force the men to have a peace, well then,　　　130
　　we must give up . . .

MYRRHINE [interrupting]
　　　　　　　　Give up what? Tell us!

LYSISTRATA
　　Then, will you do it?

MYRRHINE
　　　　　　　　Of course, we'll do it,
　　even if we have to die.

LYSISTRATA
　　　　　　　　All right then—
　　we have to give up all male penises.　　　　　–

[The women react with general consternation]

　　Why do you turn away? Where are you going?
　　How come you bite your lips and shake your heads?
　　And why so pale? How come you're crying like that?
　　Will you do it or not? What will it be?

MYRRHINE
　　I won't do it. So let the war drag on.

CALONICE
　　I won't either. The war can keep on going.　　　140　　　[130]

LYSISTRATA
　　How can you say that, you flatfish? Just now
　　you said they could slice you into halves.

CALONICE
　　Ask what you like, but not that! If I had to,
　⌜ I'd be willing to walk through fire—sooner that
　⌞ than give up screwing. There's nothing like it,
　　dear Lysistrata.

---

[1] . . . Taygetus. a high mountain in the Peloponnese.

LYSISTRATA

And what about you?

MYRRHINE
I'd choose the fire, too.

LYSISTRATA

What a debased race
we women are! It's no wonder men write
tragedies about us. We're good for nothing
but humping Poseidon in the bath tub.   150
But my Spartan friend, if you were willing,   [140]
just you and me, we still could pull it off.
So help me out.

LAMPITO

By the twin gods, it's hard
for women to sleep all by themselves
without a throbbing cock. But we must try.
We've got to have a peace.

LYSISTRATA

O you're a true friend!
The only real woman in this bunch.

CALONICE
If we really do give up what you say—
I hope it never happens!—would doing that
make peace more likely?

LYSISTRATA

By the two goddesses, yes,   160
much more likely. If we sit around at home
with all our make up on and in those gowns
made of Amorgos silk, naked underneath,   [150]
with our crotches neatly plucked, our husbands
will get stiff and want to hump. But then,
if we stay away and won't come near them,
they'll make peace soon enough. I'm sure of it.

LAMPITO
Yes, just like they say—when Menelaus

saw Helen's naked tits, he dropped his sword.[1]

CALONICE
But my friend, what if our men ignore us?   170

LYSISTRATA
Well then, in the words of Pherecrates,
you'll find another way to skin the dog.[2]

CALONICE
But fake penises aren't any use at all.   ━
What if they grab us and haul us by force   [160]
into the bedroom?

LYSISTRATA
               Just grab the door post.

CALONICE
And if they beat us?

LYSISTRATA
             Then you must submit—
but do it grudgingly, don't cooperate.
There's no enjoyment for them when they just
force it in. Besides, there are other ways
to make them suffer. They'll soon surrender.   180
No husband ever had a happy life
if he did not cooperate with his wife.

CALONICE
Well, if you two think it's good, we do, too.

LAMPITO
I'm sure we can persuade our men to work
for a just peace in everything, no tricks.
But how will you convince the Athenian mob?   [170]
They're mad for war.

---

[1] *... naked tits.* In a famous story, Menelaus went storming through Troy looking for his wife, Helen, in order to kill her. But when he found her, he was so overcome by her beauty that he relented and took her back home to Sparta.

[2] *Pherecrates:* an Athenian comic dramatist. The line may be a quotation from one of his plays.

15

LYSISTRATA

That's not your worry.
We'll win them over.

LAMPITO

I don't think so—
not while they have those triremes under sail
and that huge treasure of theirs stashed away   190
up there, where your goddess makes her home.[1]

LYSISTRATA
But that's all been well taken care of.
Today we'll capture the Acropolis.
The old women have been assigned the task.
While we sit here planning all the details,
they'll pretend they're going there to sacrifice
and seize the place.

LAMPITO

You've got it all worked out.   [180]
What you say sounds good.

LYSISTRATA

All right Lampito,
let's swear an oath as quickly as we can.
That way we'll be united.

LAMPITO

Recite the oath.   200
Then we'll all swear to it.

LYSISTRATA

That's good advice.
Where's that girl from Scythia?

[The Scythian slave steps forward. She's holding a small shield]

Why stare like that?
Put down your shield, the hollow part on top.
Now, someone get me a victim's innards.

CALONICE
Lysistrata, what sort of oath is this

[1] *. . . where your goddess makes her home.* The financial reserves of the Athenian state
were stored in the Acropolis.

16

we're going to swear?

LYSISTRATA

                           What sort of oath?
One on a shield, just like they did back then
in Aeschylus' play—with slaughtered sheep.

CALONICE

You can't, Lysistrata, not on a shield,
you can't swear an oath for peace on that.   210   [190]

LYSISTRATA

What should the oath be, then?

CALONICE

                           Let's get a stallion,
a white one, and then offer up its guts!

LYSISTRATA

Why a white horse?

CALONICE

                    How else would one swear an oath?

LYSISTRATA

I'll tell you, by god, if you want to hear.
Put a large dark bowl down here on the ground,
then sacrifice a jug of Thasian wine,
and swear we'll never pour in water.

LAMPITO

Now, if you ask me, that's a splendid oath!

LYSISTRATA

Someone get the bowl and a jug of wine.

*[The Scythian girl goes back in the house and returns with a bowl and
a jug of wine. Calonice takes the bowl]*

CALONICE

Look, dear ladies, at this splendid bowl.   220   [200]
Just touching this gives instant pleasure.

LYSISTRATA

Put it down. Now join me and place your hands
on our sacrificial victim.

17

[The women gather around the bowl and lay their hands on the wine jug. Lysistrata starts the ritual prayer]

O you,
Goddess of Persuasion and the bowl
which we so love, accept this sacrifice,
a women's offering, and be kind to us.

[Lysistrata opens the wine jug and lets the wine pour out into the bowl]

CALONICE
Such healthy blood spurts out so beautifully!

LAMPITO
By Castor, that's a mighty pleasant smell.

MYRRHINE
Ladies, let me be the first to swear the oath.

CALONICE
No, by Aphrodite, no—not unless   230
your lot is drawn.

LYSISTRATA *[holding up a bowl full of wine]*
                    Grab the brim, Lampito,
you and all the others. Someone repeat   [210]
for all the rest of you the words I say—
that way you'll pledge your firm allegiance:
No man, no husband and no lover . . .

CALONICE *[taking the oath]*
No man, no husband and no lover . . .

LYSISTRATA
. . . will get near me with a stiff prick . . . Come on,
say it!

CALONICE
              . . . will get near me with a stiff prick.
O Lysistrata, my knees are getting weak!

LYSISTRATA
At home I'll live completely without sex . . .   240

CALONICE
At home I'll live completely without sex . . .

18

LYSISTRATA
... wearing saffron silks, with lots of make up ...

CALONICE
... wearing saffron silks, with lots of make up ...   [220]

LYSISTRATA
... to make my man as horny as I can.

CALONICE
... to make my man as horny as I can.

LYSISTRATA
I'll never willingly give in to him.

CALONICE
I'll never willingly give in to him.

LYSISTRATA
If against my will he takes me by force ...

CALONICE
If against my will he takes me by force ...

LYSISTRATA
... I'll be a lousy lay, not move a limb.   250

CALONICE
... I'll be a lousy lay, not move a limb.

LYSISTRATA
I'll not raise my slippers up towards the roof ...

CALONICE
I'll not raise my slippers up towards the roof ...   [230]

LYSISTRATA
... nor crouch down like a lioness on all fours.

CALONICE
... nor crouch down like a lioness on all fours.

LYSISTRATA
If I do all this, then I may drink this wine.

CALONICE
If I do all this, then I may drink this wine.

LYSISTRATA
If I fail, may this glass fill with water.

CALONICE
If I fail, may this glass fill with water.

LYSISTRATA
All you women swear to keep this oath?

ALL
                              We do.   260

LYSISTRATA
All right. I'll make the offering.

[Lysistrata drinks some of the wine in the bowl]

CALONICE
                              Just your share,
    my dear, so we all stay firm friends.

[A sound of shouting is heard from offstage]

LAMPITO
                              What's that noise?   [240]

LYSISTRATA
    It's what I said just now—the women
    have already captured the Acropolis.
    So, Lampito, you return to Sparta—
    do good work among your people there.
    Leave these women here as hostages.
    We'll join the others in the citadel
    and help them barricade the doors.

CALONICE
    Don't you think the men will band together   270
    and march against us—and quickly, too?

LYSISTRATA
    I'm not so worried about them. They'll come
    carrying their torches and making threats,
    but they'll not pry these gates of ours apart,   [250]
    not unless they agree to our demands.

20

CALONICE
Yes, by Aphrodite, that's right. If not,
we'll be labelled weak and gutless women.

*[The women enter the citadel. The Chorus of Old Men enters slowly,
for they are quite decrepit. They are carrying wood for a fire, glowing
coals to start the blaze, and torches to light.]*

LEADER OF MEN'S CHORUS
Keep moving, Draces, pick up the pace,
even if your shoulder's tired lugging
all this heavy fresh-cut olive wood.   280

CHORUS OF OLD MEN
Alas, so many unexpected things
take place in a long life. O Strymodorus,
who'd ever think they'd hear such news
about our women—the ones we fed   [260]
in our own homes are truly bad.
The sacred statue is in their hands.
They've seized my own Acropolis
and block the doors with bolts and bars.

LEADER OF MEN'S CHORUS
Come on Philurgus, let's hurry there
as fast as we can go up to the city.   290
We'll set these logs down in a circle,
stack them so we keep them bottled up,
those women who've combined to do this.
Then with our own hands we'll set alight
a single fire and, as we all agreed
in the vote we took, we'll burn them all,
beginning first with Lycon's wife.[1]   [270]

CHORUS OF OLD MEN
They'll won't be making fun of me,
by Demeter, not while I'm still alive.
That man Cleomenes, who was the first   300
to take our citadel, went tamely back.
Snorting Spartan pride he crept away,
once he'd handed me his weapons,

---

[1] *. . . Lycon's wife:* a woman in Athens famous for her promiscuity.

21

wearing a really tiny little cloak,
hungry, filthy, with his hairy face.
He'd gone six years without a bath.[1]   [280]
That's how I fiercely hemmed him in,
our men in ranks of seventeen.
We even slept before the gates.
So with these foes of all the gods   310
and of Euripides, as well,
will I not check their insolence?
If I do not, then let my trophies
all disappear from Marathon.[2]
The rest of the trip I have to make
is uphill to the Acropolis.
We must move fast, but how to haul
this wood up there without a mule?
This pair of logs makes my shoulders sore.
But still we've got to soldier on   320
giving our fire air to breathe.
It may go out when I'm not looking,
just as I reach my journey's end.

*[They blow on the coals to keep them alight. The smoke comes
blowing up in their faces. The Old Men fall back, coughing and rub-
bing their eyes]*

           O the smoke!
Lord Hercules, how savagely
it jumped out from the pot right in my face
and bit my eyes like a raving bitch.
It works just like a Lemnian fire,   [300]
or else it wouldn't use its teeth
to feed on fluids in my eye.
We need to hurry to the citadel   330
and save the goddess. If not now,

[1] *Cleomenes*, a king of Sparta, once came with a small army to Athens (in 508 BC). He
had a very hostile reception and took refuge in the Acropolis, where he stayed under
siege for two days. A truce was arranged and the Spartans left peacefully.

[2] *. . . from Marathon*: Euripides is the famous tragic dramatist, a younger contemporary
of Aristophanes. Marathon was the site of the great Greek victory of the Persian expedi-
tionary forces in 490 BC, a high point of Athenian military achievement.

O Laches, when should we help her out? [1]

[The men blow on the coals and are again overpowered by the smoke]

Damn and blast this smoke!

LEADER OF MEN'S CHORUS
Thanks to the gods, the fire's up again —
a lively flame. So what if, first of all,
we placed our firewood down right here, then put
a vine branch in the pot, set it alight,
and charged the door like a battering ram?
We'll order women to remove the bars   [310]
and, if they refuse, burn down the doors.   340
We'll overpower them with the smoke.
All right, put down your loads.

[The men set down their logs. Once again the smoke is too much for them]

                    This bloody smoke!
Is there any general here from Samos
who'll help us with this wood? [2]

[He sets down his load of wood]

                    Ah, that's better.
They're not shrinking my spine any more.
All right, pot, it's now your job to rouse up
a fire from those coals, so first of all,
I'll have a lighted torch and lead the charge.
O lady Victory, stand with us here,
so we can set our trophy up in there,   350
defeat those women in our citadel,
put down this present insolence of theirs.

[The Old Men stack their logs in a pile and start lighting their torches on the coals. The Chorus of Old Women enters. They are carrying pitchers of water]

[1] . . . *help her out*: The reference to Lemnian fire is not clear. The island of Lemnos perhaps had some volcanic activity, or else the reference is to the women of Lemnos who killed all their husbands.

[2] . . . *Samos*: Samos is an important island near Athens. A number of the generals of Athenian forces came from there.

23

LEADER OF WOMEN'S CHORUS
    Ladies, I think I see some flames and smoke,
    as if a fire was burning. We'd better hurry.   [320]

CHORUS OF OLD WOMEN
    We have to fly, Nicodice, fly
    before Critylla is burned up
    and Calyce, too, by nasty winds
    and old men keen to wipe them out.
    But I'm afraid I'll be too late
    to help them out. I've only just   360
    filled up my pitcher in the dark.
    It was not easy—at the well
    the place was jammed and noisy too,
    with clattering pots, pushy servants,
    and tattooed slaves. But I was keen
    to carry water to these fires
    to help my country's women out.
    I've heard some dim and dull old men
    are creeping here and carrying logs—
    a great big load—to our fortress,   370
    as if to warm our public baths.
    They're muttering the most awful things
    how with their fire they need to turn   [340]
    these hateful women into ash.
    But, goddess, may I never see
    them burned like that—but witness how
    they rescue cities, all of Greece,
    from war and this insanity.
    That's why, golden-crested goddess
    who guards our city, these women   380
    have now occupied your shrine.
    O Tritogeneia, I summon you
    to be my ally—if any man
    sets them on fire, help us out
    as we carry this water up to them.[1]

*[The Old Men have lit their torches and are about to move against the
Acropolis. The Old Women move to block their way]*

---

[1] *Tritogenia* is a common name for the goddess Athena. Its precise meaning is unclear
("Trito born").

LEADER OF WOMEN'S CHORUS
Hold on, ladies. What this I see? Men—   [350]
dirty old men—hard at work. Honest types,
useful, god-fearing men, could never do
the things you do.

LEADER OF MEN'S CHORUS
    What's happening here
is something we did not expect to see—   390
a swarm of women standing here like this
to guard the doors.

LEADER OF WOMEN'S CHORUS
    So you're afraid of us?
Do we look like an enormous crowd?
You're seeing just a fraction of our size—
there are ten thousand more.

LEADER OF MEN'S CHORUS
    Hey there, Phaedrias!
Shall we stop her nattering on like this?
Someone hit her, smack her with a log.

LEADER OF WOMEN'S CHORUS
Let's put our water jugs down on the ground,
in case they want to lay their hands on us.
Down there they won't get in our way.   400

[The Old Women set down their water jugs]

LEADER OF MEN'S CHORUS
By god, someone should hit them on the jaw,   [360]
two or three times, and then, like Boupalus,
they'll won't have anything much more to say.[1]

LEADER OF WOMEN'S CHORUS
Come on then—strike me. I'm here, waiting.
No other bitch will ever grab your balls.

LEADER OF MEN'S CHORUS
Shut up, or I'll hit you—snuff out your old age.

---

[1] *. . . much more to say*: Boupalus was a sculptor from Chios.

LEADER OF WOMEN'S CHORUS
  Try coming up and touching Stratyllis
  with your finger tips!

LEADER OF MEN'S CHORUS
                    What if I thrashed you
  with my fists? Would you do something nasty?

LEADER OF WOMEN'S CHORUS
  With my teeth I'll rip out your lungs and guts!   410

LEADER OF MEN'S CHORUS
  Euripides is such a clever poet—
  ⌈ the man who says there's no wild animal
  ⌊ more shameless than a woman.

LEADER OF WOMEN'S CHORUS
                    Come on then,
  Rhodippe, let's pick up our water jugs.   [370]

[The Old Women pick up their water jugs again]

LEADER OF MEN'S CHORUS
  Why have you damned women even come here
  carrying this water?

LEADER OF WOMEN'S CHORUS
                    And why are you
  bringing fire, you old corpse? Do you intend
  to set yourselves alight?

LEADER OF MEN'S CHORUS
              Me? To start a blaze
  and roast your friends.

LEADER OF WOMEN'S CHORUS
              I'm here to douse your fire.

LEADER OF MEN'S CHORUS
  You'll put out my fire?

LEADER OF WOMEN'S CHORUS
                    Yes I will. You'll see.   420

LEADER OF MEN'S CHORUS *[waving his torch]*
  I don't know why I'm not just doing it,

26

frying you in this flame.

LEADER OF WOMEN'S CHORUS
                    Get yourself some soap.
I'm giving you a bath.

LEADER OF MEN'S CHORUS
                    You'll wash me,
you old wrinkled prune?

LEADER OF WOMEN'S CHORUS
                    Yes, it will be
just like your wedding night.

LEADER OF MEN'S CHORUS
                    Listen to her!
She's a nervy bitch!

LEADER OF WOMEN'S CHORUS
                    I'm a free woman.

LEADER OF MEN'S CHORUS
I'll make you shut up!

LEADER OF WOMEN'S CHORUS
                    You don't judge these things.   [380]

LEADER OF MEN'S CHORUS
Set her hair on fire!

LEADER OF WOMEN'S CHORUS
                    Get to work, Achelous.[1]

[She throws her jar of water over the Leader of the Men's Chorus, and, following the leader's example, the women throw water all over the old men]

LEADER OF MEN'S CHORUS
O, that's bad!

LEADER OF WOMEN'S CHORUS
                    Was that hot enough?

[The women continue to throw water on the old men]

---

[1] *. . . to work, Achelous.* The Achelous was a large river in northern Greece.

27

LEADER OF MEN'S CHORUS

                         Hot enough?
Won't you stop doing that? What are you doing?   430

LEADER OF WOMEN'S CHORUS
I'm watering you to make you bloom.

LEADER OF MEN'S CHORUS
I'm too old and withered. I'm shaking.

LEADER OF WOMEN'S CHORUS
Well, you've got your fire. Warm yourselves up.

[A Magistrate enters with an armed escort of four public guards and slaves with crowbars and some attendant soldiers]

MAGISTRATE
Has not our women's lewdness shown itself
in how they beat their drums for Sabazius,
that god of excess, or on their rooftops
shed tears for Adonis? That's what I heard   [390]
one time in our assembly. Demostrates—
what a stupid man he is!—was arguing
that we should sail to Sicily. Meanwhile,   440
his wife was dancing round and screaming out
"Alas, Adonis!" While Demostrates talked,
saying we should levy soldiers from Zacynthus,
the woman was on the roof top, getting drunk
and yelling out "Weep for Adonis! Weep!" [1]
But he kept on forcing his opinion through,
that mad brutal ox, whom the gods despise.
That's just the kind of loose degenerate stuff
that comes from women.

LEADER OF MEN'S CHORUS
                  Wait until I tell you
the insolent things these women did to us—   450
all their abuse—they dumped their water jugs   [400]

---

[1] *. . . Weep!*: Sabazius was a popular foreign god associated with drinking (like Dionysus). Adonis was a mortal youth loved by Aphrodite. An annual festival was celebrated in his memory. Demostrates was a politician promoting the disastrous Athenian military expedition to Sicily. Zacynthus is an island off the Peloponnese, an ally of Athens.

28

on us. So now we have to dry our clothes.
We look as if we've pissed ourselves.

MAGISTRATE
                              By Poseidon,
god of the salt seas, it serves you right.
We men ourselves share in the blame for this.
We teach our wives their free and easy life,
and so intrigues come flowering out from them.
Here's what we tell some working artisan,
"O goldsmith, about that necklace I bought here—
last night my wife was dancing and the bolt   460   [410]
slipped from its hole. I have to take a boat
to Salamis. If you've got time tonight,
you could visit her with that tool of yours
and fix the way the bolt sits in her hole."
Another man goes to the shoemaker,
a strapping lad with an enormous prick,
and says, "O shoemaker, a sandal strap
is pinching my wife's tender little toe.
Could you come at noon and rub her strap,
stretch it really wide?" That's the sort of thing   470   [420]
that leads to all this trouble. Look at me,
a magistrate in charge of finding oars
and thus in need of money now—these women
have shut the treasury doors to keep me out.
But standing here's no use.

[He calls out to his two slaves]

                              Bring the crow bars.
I'll stop these women's insolence myself.

[He turns to the armed guards he has brought with him]

What are you gaping at, you idiot!
And you—what are you looking at?
Why are you doing nothing—just staring round
looking for a tavern? Take these crowbars   480
to the doors there, and then pry them open.
Come, I'll work to force them open with you.

29

LYSISTRATA *[opening the doors and walking out]*
No need to use those crowbars. I'm coming out—   [430]
and of my own free will. Why these crowbars?
This calls for brains and common sense, not force.

MAGISTRATE
Is that so, you slut? Where's that officer?
Seize that woman! Tie her hands!

LYSISTRATA
                    By Artemis,
he may be a public servant, but if
he lays a finger on me, he'll be sorry.

MAGISTRATE *[to the first armed guard]*
Are you scared of her? Grab her round the waist!   490
You there, help him out! And tie her up!

OLD WOMAN A[1]
By Pandrosus, if you lift a hand to her,
I'll beat you until you shit yourself!   [440]

[The two armed guards trying to grab Lysistrata are so terrified they shit themselves]

MAGISTRATE
Look at the mess you made! Where is he,
that other officer?

[The Magistrate turns to a third armed officer]

                    Tie up this one first,
the one who's got such a filthy mouth.

OLD WOMAN B
By the god of light, if you just touch her,
you'll quickly need a cup to fix your eyes.[2]

[This officer runs off. The Magistrate turns to a fourth officer]

[1]OLD WOMAN A: In many modern productions the old women who speak in this scene either come out of the gates to the Acropolis or are members of the Chorus. Alternatively the speeches could be assigned to the characters we have met earlier (Myrrhine and Calonice), who emerge from the Acropolis behind Lysistrata.

[2]... *fix your eyes.* Black eyes were treated with a small cup placed over the eye to reduce the swelling.

MAGISTRATE
Who's this here? Arrest her! I'll put a stop
to all women in this demonstration!   500

OLD WOMAN C
By bull-bashing Artemis, if you move
to touch her, I'll rip out all your hair
until you yelp in pain.

[The fourth officer runs off in terror]

MAGISTRATE
                              This is getting bad.
There are no officers left. We can't let ourselves   [450]
be beaten back by women. Come on then,
you Scythians, form up your ranks.[1] Then charge.
Go at them!

LYSISTRATA
                    By the two goddesses, you'll see—
we've got four companies of women inside,
all fighting fit and fully armed.

MAGISTRATE
                                        Come on,
Scythians, twist their arms behind them!   510

LYSISTRATA *[shouting behind her]*
Come out here from where you are in there,
all you female allies, on the double—
you market women who sell grain and eggs,
garlic and vegetables, and those who run
our bakeries and taverns, to the attack!

[Many women emerge from the Acropolis, armed in various ways]

Hit them, stomp on them, scratch their eyeballs,
cover them with your abuse! Don't hold back!   [460]

*[A general tumult occurs in which the women beat back the Scythian
guards]*

---

[1] *Scythians.* The armed guards accompanying the Magistrate are traditionally Scythian
archers.

LYSISTRATA

    That's enough! Back off! Don't strip the armour
    from those you have defeated.

MAGISTRATE

                              Disaster!
    My guards have acted quite disgracefully.   520

LYSISTRATA

    What did you expect? Did you really think
    you were facing a bunch of female slaves?
    Or is it your belief that mere women
    have no spirit in them?

MAGISTRATE

                    Spirit? By Apollo, yes!
    If they're near any man who's got some wine.

LEADER OF MEN'S CHORUS

    In this land you're a magistrate, but here
    your words are useless. Why even try
    to have a conversation with these bitches?
    Don't you know they've just given us a bath
    in our own cloaks? And they did not use soap!   530   [470]

LEADER OF WOMEN'S CHORUS

    Listen, friend. You should never raise your hand
    against your neighbour. If you do, then I
    will have to punch you in the eye. I'd prefer
    to sit quietly at home, like a young girl,
    and not come here to injure anyone
    or agitate the nest, unless someone
    disturbs the hive and makes me angry.

CHORUS OF OLD MEN

    O Zeus, however will we find a way
    to deal with these wild beasts? What's going on
    is no longer something we can bear.   540
    But we must question them and find out why
    they are so angry with us, why they wish   [480]
    to seize the citadel of Cranaus,
    the holy ground where people do not go,

on the great rock of the Acropolis.[1]

LEADER OF THE MEN'S CHORUS *[to Magistrate]*
So ask her. Don't let them win you over.
Challenge everything they say. If we left
this matter without seeking out the cause
that would be disgraceful.

MAGISTRATE *[turning to Lysistrata]*
                Well then, by god,
first of all I'd like to know the reason   550
why you planned to use these barriers here
to barricade our citadel.

LYSISTRATA
                To get your money
so you couldn't keep on paying for war.

MAGISTRATE
Is it money that's the cause of war?

LYSISTRATA
Yes, and all the rest of the corruption.
Peisander and our leading politicians   [490]
need a chance to steal. That's the reason
they're always stirring up disturbances.[2]
Well, let the ones who wish to do this
do what they want, but from this moment on   560
they'll get no more money.

MAGISTRATE
                What will you do?

LYSISTRATA
You ask me that? We'll control it.

MAGISTRATE
                You mean
you're going to manage all the money?

---

[1] *. . . of the Acropolis.* Cranaus was a legendary king of Athens.

[2] *. . . up disturbances.* Peisander was a leading Athenian politician, suspected of favouring the war for selfish reasons.

LYSISTRATA
　　You consider that so strange?　Isn't it true
　　we take care of all the household money?

MAGISTRATE
　　That's not the same.

LYSISTRATA
　　　　　　　　Why not?

MAGISTRATE
　　　　　　　　　　　We need the cash
　　to carry on the war.

LYSISTRATA
　　　　　　　　　　Well, first of all,
　　there should be no fighting.

MAGISTRATE
　　　　　　　　　　But without war
　　how will we save ourselves?

LYSISTRATA
　　　　　　　　We'll do that.

MAGISTRATE
　　　　　　　　　　　　You?

LYSISTRATA
　　That's right—us.

MAGISTRATE
　　　　　　　　This is outrageous!

LYSISTRATA
　　　　　　　　　　　We'll save you,　　　　570
　　even if that goes against your wishes.

MAGISTRATE
　　What you're saying is madness!

LYSISTRATA
　　　　　　　　　　You're angry,
　　but nonetheless we have to do it.

MAGISTRATE
　　By Demeter, this is against the law!　　　　[500]

34

LYSISTRATA
My dear fellow, we have to rescue you.

MAGISTRATE
And if I don't agree?

LYSISTRATA
                              Then our reasons
are that much more persuasive.

MAGISTRATE
                                        Is it true
you're really going to deal with peace and war?

LYSISTRATA
We're going to speak to that.

MAGISTRATE *[with a threatening gesture]*
                              Then speak fast,
or else you may well start to cry.

LYSISTRATA
                              Then listen—   580
and try to keep your fists controlled.

MAGISTRATE
                              I can't.
It's hard for me to hold back my temper.

LEADER OF WOMEN'S CHORUS
It's more likely you're the one who'll weep.

MAGISTRATE
Shut up your croaking, you old bag.

[To Lysistrata]

                              You—talk to me.

LYSISTRATA
I'll do that. Up to now through this long war
we kept silent about all those things
you men were doing. We were being modest.
And you did not allow us to speak up,
although we were not happy. But still,
we listened faithfully to you, and often   590   [510]

inside the house we heard your wretched plans
for some great deed. And if we ached inside,
we'd force a smile and simply ask, "Today
in the assembly did the men propose
a treaty carved in stone decreeing peace?"
But our husbands said, "Is that your business?
Why don't you shut up?" And I'd stay silent.

OLD WOMAN
I'd not have kept my mouth shut.

MAGISTRATE *[to Lysistrata]*
                                        You'd have been smacked
if you hadn't been quiet and held your tongue.

LYSISTRATA
So there I am at home, saying nothing.   600
Then you'd tell us of another project,
even stupider than before. We'd say,
"How can you carry out a scheme like that?
It's foolish." Immediately he'd frown
and say to me, "If you don't spin your thread,
you'll get a major beating on your head.   [520]
War is men's concern."

MAGISTRATE
                                        Yes, by god!
That man spoke the truth.

LYSISTRATA
                                        You idiot!
Is that sensible—not to take advice
when what you're proposing is so silly?   610
Then we heard you speaking in the streets,
asking openly, "Are there any men
still left here in our land?" and someone said,
"By god, there's no one." Well then, after that
it seemed to us we had to rescue Greece
by bringing wives into a single group
with one shared aim. Why should we delay?
If you'd like to hear us give some good advice,
then keep your mouths shut and start to listen,
the way we did. We'll save you from yourselves.   620

36

MAGISTRATE
You'll save us? What you're saying is madness.
I'm not going to put up with it!

LYSISTRATA
                    Be quiet!

MAGISTRATE
Should I shut up for you, you witch, someone   [530]
with a scarf around her head? I'd sooner die!

LYSISTRATA
If this scarf of mine really bothers you,
take it and wrap it round your head. Here—

[Lysistrata takes off her scarf and wraps it over the Magistrate's head.]

    Now keep quiet!

OLD WOMAN A
                    And take this basket, too!

LYSISTRATA
Now put on a waist band, comb out wool,
and chew some beans. This business of the war
we women will take care of.

LEADER OF WOMEN'S CHORUS
                        Come on, women,   630
get up and leave those jars. It's our turn now   [540]
to join together with our friends.

WOMEN'S CHORUS
With dancing I'll never tire—
weariness won't grip my knees
or wear me out. In everything
I'll strive to match the excellence
these women here possess—in nature,
wisdom, boldness, charm,
and prudent virtue in the way
they love their country.   640

LEADER OF WOMEN'S CHORUS
You grandchildren of the bravest women,
sprung from fruitful stinging nettles,

37

let your passion drive you forward,
and don't be shy, for now you've got
the winds of fortune at your back.   [550]

LYSISTRATA
⌈ O Aphrodite born on Cyprus
│ and, you, sweet passionate Eros, breathe
│ sexual longing on our breasts and thighs
│ and fill our men with tortuous desire
│ and make their pricks erect. If so, I think   650
│ we'll win ourselves a name among the Greeks
⌊ as those who brought an end to warfare.

MAGISTRATE
What will you do?

LYSISTRATA
                            For a start, we'll stop
you men hanging around the market place
armed with spears and acting up like fools.

OLD WOMAN A
Yes, that's right, by Paphian Aphrodite!

LYSISTRATA
Right now in the market they stroll around
among the pots and vegetables, fully armed,
like Corybantes.[1]

MAGISTRATE
                            Yes, that's right—
it's what brave men should do.

LYSISTRATA
                            It looks so silly—   660
going off to purchase tiny little birds
while carrying a Gorgon shield.[2]   [560]

OLD WOMAN A
                            By god,
I myself saw a cavalry commander—

---

[1] *Corybantes* were divine attendants on the foreign goddess Cybele.

[2] *. . . Gorgon shield*: Shields with monstrous Gorgon heads depicted on them were
common in Athens.

he had long hair and was on horseback—
pouring out some pudding he'd just bought
from an old woman into his helmet.
Another Thracian was waving his spear
and his shield, as well, just like Tereus,
and terrifying the woman selling figs
while gobbling down the ripest ones she had.[1]   670

MAGISTRATE
And how will you find the power to stop
so many violent disturbances
throughout our states and then resolve them?

LYSISTRATA
Very easily.

MAGISTRATE
                    But how? Explain that.

LYSISTRATA
It's like a bunch of yarn. When it's tangled,
we take it and pass it through the spindle
back and forth—that's how we'll end the war,
if people let us try, by sending out   [570]
ambassadors here and there, back and forth.

MAGISTRATE
You're an idiot! Do you really think   680
you can end such fearful acts with spindles,
spools, and wool?

LYSISTRATA
                    If you had any common sense,
you'd deal with everything the way we do
when we handle yarn.

MAGISTRATE
                    What does that mean?
Tell me.

LYSISTRATA
                    First of all, just as we wash the wool
in a rinsing tub to remove the dirt,

---

[1] *Tereus* was a mythical king of Thrace and a popular figure with Athenian dramatists.

you have to lay the city on a bed,
beat out the rascals, and then drive away
the thorns and break apart the groups of men
who join up together in their factions   690
seeking public office—pluck out their heads.
Then into a common basket of good will
comb out the wool, the entire compound mix,
including foreigners, guests, and allies,   [580]
anyone useful to the public good.
Bundle them together. As for those cities
which are colonies of this land, by god,
you must see that, as far as we're concerned,
each is a separate skein. From all of them,
take a piece of wool and bring it here.   700
Roll them together into a single thing.
Then you'll have made one mighty ball of wool,
from which the public then must weave its clothes.

MAGISTRATE
So women beat wool, roll it up in balls!
Isn't that wonderful? That doesn't mean
they bear any part of what goes on in war.

LYSISTRATA
You silly fool, of course it does—we endure
more than twice as much as you. First of all,
we bear children and then send them off
to serve as soldiers.

MAGISTRATE
                        All right, be quiet.   710   [590]
Don't remind me of all that.

LYSISTRATA
                        And then,
when we should be having a good time,
enjoying our youth, we have to sleep alone
because our men are in the army.
Setting us aside, it distresses me
that young unmarried girls are growing old
alone in their own homes.

MAGISTRATE
                    Don't men get old?

LYSISTRATA
  By god, that's not the same at all. For men,
  even old ones with white hair, can come back
  and quickly marry some young girl. For women   720
  time soon runs out. If they don't seize their chance,
  no one wants to marry them—they sit there
  waiting for an oracle.

MAGISTRATE
                    But an old man
  who can still get his prick erect . . .

LYSISTRATA *[interrupting]*
                                O you—
  why not learn your lesson and just die? It's time.   [600]
  Buy a funeral urn. I'll prepare the dough
  for honey cakes.[1] Take this wreath.

[Lysistrata throws some water over the Magistrate]

OLD WOMAN A
                    This one, too —
  it's from me!

[Old Woman A throws more water on the Magistrate]

OLD WOMAN B
          Here, take this garland!

[Old Woman B throws more water on the Magistrate]

LYSISTRATA
                    Well now,
  what do you need? What are you waiting for?
  Step aboard the boat. Charon's calling you.   730
  You're preventing him from casting off.[2]

---

[1] *Honey cakes* were traditionally part of the funeral service, given to make sure the dead shade reached Hades.

[2] *Charon* was the ferryman who transported the shades of the dead across the river into Hades.

MAGISTRATE
I don't have to put up with these insults!
I'll go to the other magistrates, by god,
and show myself exactly as I am! [620]

[The Magistrate exits with his attending slaves]

LYSISTRATA *[calling out to him as he leaves]*
Are you blaming us for not laying you out
for burial? Well then, on the third day,
we'll come and offer up a sacrifice
on your behalf first thing in the morning.

[Lysistrata and the old women with her return inside the Acropolis]

LEADER OF THE MEN'S CHORUS
You men, no more sleeping on the job
for anyone born free! Let's strip ourselves 740
for action on this issue. It seems to me
this business stinks—it's large and getting larger.

[The Old Men strip down, taking almost all their clothes off]

CHORUS OF OLD MEN
And I especially smelled some gas—
the tyrant rule of Hippias.
I've a great fear that Spartan men
collected here with Cleisthenes,
have with their trickery stirred up
these women, whom the gods all hate,
to seize the treasury and our pay,
the funds I need to live my way.[1] 750
It's terrible these women here
are thinking about politics
and prattling on about bronze spears—
they're women!—and making peace
on our behalf with Spartan types,
whom I don't trust, not any more
than gaping wolves. In this affair,
those men are weaving plots for us, [630]

[1] *Hippias* was a tyrant in Athens from 528 to 510. *Cleisthenes*, an Athenian, was a favourite target of Aristophanes, ridiculed as a passive homosexual. The pay the old men refer to is a daily allowance of three obols to jury men.

so they can bring back tyranny.
But me, I won't give any ground,   760
not to a tyrant. I'll stand guard,
from now on carrying a sword
inside my myrtle bough. I'll march
with weapons in the market place
with Aristogeiton at my side.[1]
I'll stand with him. And now it's time
I struck those hostile to gods' law
and hit that old hag on the jaw.

[The Old Men move to threaten the Old Women with their fists]

LEADER OF WOMEN'S CHORUS
    When you get back home, your own mother
    won't know who you are. Come on, old ladies,   770
    you friends of mine, let's first set our burdens
    on the ground.

WOMEN'S CHORUS
                    All you fellow citizens,
    we'll start to give the city good advice
    and rightly, since it raised us splendidly   [640]
    so we lived very well. At seven years old,
    I carried sacred vessels, and at ten
    I pounded barley for Athena's shrine.
    Later as bear, I shed my yellow dress
    for the rites of Brauronian Artemis.
    And once I was a lovely full-grown girl,   780
    I wore strings of figs around my neck
    and was one of those who carried baskets.
    So I am indebted to the city.
    Why not pay it back with good advice?[2]
    I was born a woman, but don't hold that
    against me if I introduce a plan
    to make our present situation better.   [650]

---

[1] *Aristogeiton*. One of the two men who led the attack on the Athenian tyrants and thus became a symbol of the highest democratic ideals in the city.

[2] The Old Women in these lines are referring to many city activities and rituals in which girls of noble families played important roles. The phrase "as bear" refers to a ritual in honour of Artemis.

43

For I make contributions to the state—
I give birth to men. You miserable old farts,
you contribute nothing! That pile of cash   790
which we collected from the Persian Wars
you squandered. You don't pay any taxes.
What's more, the way you act so stupidly
endangers all of us. What do you say?
Don't get me riled up. I'll take this filthy shoe
and smack you one right on the jaw.

CHORUS OF OLD MEN
Is this not getting way too insolent?
I think it's better if we paid them back.   [660]
We have to fight this out. So any one
who's got balls enough to be a man   800
take off your clothes so we men can smell
the way we should—like men. We should strip.
It's not right to keep ourselves wrapped up.
We're the ones who've got white feet.
We marched to Leipsydrion years ago.[1]
And now let's stand erect again, aroused
in our whole bodies—shake off our old age.   [670]

[The Old Men take off their remaining clothes, hold up their shrivelled phalluses, and threaten the women]

If one of us gives them the slightest chance
there's nothing these women won't continue
trying to work on—building fighting ships,   810
attacking us at sea like Artemesia.[2]
If they switch to horses, I draw the line.
For women are the best at riding bareback—
their shapely arses do a lovely job.
They don't slip off when grinding at a gallop.
Just look how Micon painted Amazons

---

[1]*Leipsydrion* was the site of a battle years before when the tyrant Hippias besieged and defeated his opponents. The old men are treating the event as if they had been victorious. The detail about their white feet, Sommerstein suggests, refers to those who were hostile to Hippias and the tyrants (hence, lovers of freedom).

[2]*Artemesia* was queen of Halicarnassus in Asia Minor. She led ships from her city as part of the Persian expedition against Athens in 480 and fought at the Battle of Salamis.

fighting men on horseback hand to hand.[1]
So we must take a piece of wood with holes,   [680]
and fit a yoke on them, around their necks.

CHORUS OF OLD WOMEN
By the two goddesses, if you get me roused,   820
I'll let my wild sow's passion loose and make
you yell to all the people here today
how I'm removing all your hair.

LEADER OF WOMEN'S CHORUS
                                    You ladies,
let's not delay—let's take off all our clothes,
so we can smell a woman's passion
when we're in a ferocious mood.

[The Old Women take off their clothes]

WOMEN'S CHORUS
Now let any man step out against me—
he won't be eating garlic any more,   [690]
and no black beans. Just say something nasty,
I'm so boiling mad, I'll treat you the same way   830
the beetle did the eagle—smash your eggs.[2]

LEADER OF WOMEN'S CHORUS
Not that I give a damn for you, not while
I have Lampito here—Ismenia, too,
my young Theban friend. You have no power,
not even with seven times as many votes.
You're such a miserable old man, even those
who are you neighbours find you hateful.
Just yesterday for the feast of Hecate,   [700]
I planned a party, so I asked my neighbours
in Boeotia for one of their companions,   840
a lovely girl—she was for my children—
a splendid pot of eels. But they replied
they couldn't send it because you'd passed

---

[1] *Micon* was a well-known Athenian painter.

[2] *beetle . . . eagle.* This is a reference to an old story in which the dung beetle got its
revenge against an eagle by smashing its eggs. The old woman obviously threatens the
man's testicles as she says this.

another one of your decrees.[1] It doesn't seem
you'll stop voting in these laws, not before
someone takes your leg, carries you off
and throws you out.

*[Lysistrata comes out from the Acropolis, looking very worried and
angry. The leader of the Women's Chorus addresses her]*

        Here's our glorious leader,
who does the planning for this enterprise.
Why have you come here, outside the building,
and with such a sad expression on your face?   850

LYSISTRATA
It's the way these women act so badly,
together with their female hearts—it makes
me lose my courage and walk in circles.

LEADER OF WOMEN'S CHORUS
What are you saying? What do you mean?   [710]

LYSISTRATA
It's true, so true.

LEADER OF WOMEN'S CHORUS
        What's wrong? You can tell us—
we're friends of yours.

LYSISTRATA
        I'm ashamed to say,
but it's hard to keep it quiet.

LEADER OF WOMEN'S CHORUS
        Don't hide from me
bad news affecting all of us.

LYSISTRATA
        All right,
I'll keep it short—we all want to get laid.

LEADER OF WOMEN'S CHORUS
O Zeus!

---

[1] As noted earlier (at line 28) eels were a delicacy associated with Boeotia, a state allied
with Athens' enemies. *Hecate* was a goddess whose worship was associated with birth
and children.

46

LYSISTRATA

What's the point of calling Zeus?   860
There's nothing he can do about this mess.
I can't keep these women from their men,
not any longer—they're all running off.
First I caught one slipping through a hole   [720]
beside the Cave of Pan, then another
trying it with a rope and pulley, a third
deserting on her own, and yesterday
there was a woman on a giant bird
intending to fly down to that place
run by Orsilochus.[1] I grabbed her hair.   870
They're all inventing reasons to go home.

[A woman come out of the citadel, trying to sneak off]

Here's one of them on her way right now.
Where do you think you're going?

WOMAN A

Who me?
I want to get back home. Inside the house
I've got bolts of Milesian cloth, and worms
are eating them.

LYSISTRATA

What worms? Get back in there!   [730]

WOMAN A

I'll come back right away, by god—but now
I need to spread them on the bed.

LYSISTRATA

Spread them?
You won't be doing that. You're not leaving!

WOMAN A

My wool just goes to waste?

LYSISTRATA

If that's what it takes.   880

[Woman A trudges back into the Acropolis. Woman B emerges]

---

[1] *Orsilochus* was either a well-known seducer or someone who kept a brothel.

47

WOMAN B
I'm such a fool, I've left my wretched flax
back in my house unstripped.

LYSISTRATA
                    Another one
leaving here to go and strip her flax!
Get back inside!

WOMAN B
                    By the goddess of light,
I'll be right back, once I've rubbed its skin.

LYSISTRATA
You'll not rub anything. If you start that,   [740]
some other woman will want to do the same.

*[Woman B returns dejected into the citadel. Woman C emerges from
the citadel, looking very pregnant]*

WOMAN C
O sacred Eileithia, goddess of birth,
hold back my labour pains till I can find
a place where I'm permitted to give birth.[1]   890

LYSISTRATA
What are you moaning about?

WOMAN C
                    It's my time—
I'm going to have a child!

LYSISTRATA
                    But yesterday
you weren't even pregnant.

WOMAN C
                    Well, today I am.
Send me home, Lysistrata, and quickly.
I need a midwife.

LYSISTRATA *[inspecting Woman C's clothing]*
                    What are you saying?
What's this you've got here? It feels quite rigid.

[1] *permitted to give birth*: To have a child in a holy place was a sacrilege.

48

WOMAN C
A little boy.

LYSISTRATA
No, by Aphrodite,
I don't think so. It looks like you've got   [750]
some hollow metal here. I'll have a look.

[Lysistrata looks under the woman's dress and pulls out a helmet]

You silly creature, you've got a helmet there,   ˙   900
Athena's sacred helmet. Didn't you say
you were pregnant?

WOMAN C
Yes, and by god, I am.

LYSISTRATA
Then why've you got this helmet?

WOMAN C
Well, in case
I went into labour in the citadel.
I could give birth right in the helmet,
lay it in there like a nesting pigeon.

LYSISTRATA
What are you talking about? You're just
making an excuse—that's so obvious.
You'll stay here for at least five days
until your new child's birth is purified.   910

WOMAN C
I can't get any sleep in the Acropolis,
not since I saw the snake that guards the place.

[More women start sneaking out of the citadel]

WOMAN D
Nor can I. I'm dying from lack of sleep—   [760]
those wretched owls keep hooting all the time.

LYSISTRATA
Come on ladies, stop all these excuses!
All right, you miss your men. But don't you see
they miss you, too? I'm sure the nights they spend

don't bring them any pleasure. But please, dear friends,
hold on—persevere a little longer.
An oracle has said we will prevail,   920
if we stand together. That's what it said.

WOMAN A
Tell us what it prophesied.

LYSISTRATA
                    Then, keep quiet.
"When the sparrows, as they fly away,   [770]
escaping from the hoopoe birds, shall stay
together in one place and shall say nay
to sexual encounters, then a bad day
will be rare. High thundering Zeus will say
'What once was underneath on top I'll lay.'"

WOMAN B [interrupting]
Women are going to lie on top of men?

LYSISTRATA [continuing the oracle]
" . . . but if the sparrows fight and fly away   930
out of the holy shrine, people will say
no bird is more promiscuous than they."

WOMAN A
That oracle is clear enough, by god.

LYSISTRATA
All you heavenly gods, can we stop talking
of being in such distress. Let us go back in.
For, my dearest friends, it will be a shame
if we don't live up to this prophecy.   [780]

[Lysistrata and the women go back into the Acropolis]

MEN'S CHORUS
I'd like to tell you all a tale,
which I heard once when I was young
about Melanion, a young lad   940
who fled from marriage and then came
into the wilds. And so he lived
up in the hills. He wove some nets   [790]
and hunted hares. He had a dog.

50

Not once did he return back home
He hated women—they made him sick.
And we are no less wise than he.

LEADER OF MEN'S CHORUS
Let's kiss, old bag, give it a try.

LEADER OF WOMEN'S CHORUS
You won't need onions to make you cry.

LEADER OF MEN'S CHORUS
I'll lift my leg—give you a kick.   950

LEADER OF WOMAN'S CHORUS
Down there your pubic hair's too thick.   —   [800]

LEADER OF MEN'S CHORUS
Myronides had a hairy dick
and beat foes with his big black bum.
That Phormio was another one.[1]

WOMEN'S CHORUS
To you I'd like to tell a tale
to answer your Melanion.
There was a man called Timon once,
a vagabond, the Furies' child.
Wild thistles covered his whole face.   [810]
He wandered off filled up with spite   960
and always cursing evil types.
But though he always hated men,
especially those who are such fools,
his love for women never flagged.   [820]

LEADER OF WOMEN'S CHORUS
You'd like a punch right on the chin?

LEADER OF MEN'S CHORUS
Not given the state of fear I'm in.

LEADER OF WOMEN'S CHORUS
What if I kicked you with my toe?

LEADER OF MEN'S CHORUS
We'd see your pussy down below.

[1] *Myronides* and *Phormio* were two dead generals who fought for Athens.

51

LEADER OF WOMEN'S CHORUS
And then you'd see, although I'm old
it's not all matted hair down there,   970
but singed by lamp and plucked with flair.

[Lysistrata appears on a balcony of the citadel, looking off in the distance. Other women come out after her.]

LYSISTRATA
Hey, you women! Over here to me. Come quick!

CALONICE
What's going on? Why are you shouting?   [830]

LYSISTRATA
                                    A man!
I see a man approaching mad with love,
seized with desire for Aphrodite's rites.
O Cythera, holy queen of Cyprus
and Paphos, keep moving down the road,
the straight path you've been travelling on.

CALONICE
Where is he, whoever he is?

LYSISTRATA
                                    Over there,
right beside the shrine of Chloe.

CALONICE
                                    O yes,   980
there he is, by god. Who is he?

LYSISTRATA
                                    Have a look.
Do any of you know him?

MYRRHINE
                                    O god, I do.
It's my husband Cinesias.

LYSISTRATA
                                    All right,
your job is to torment him, be a tease,
make him hot, offer to have sex with him,   [840]

52

and then refuse, try everything you can,
except the things you swore to on the bowl.

MYRRHINE
Don't you worry. I'll do that.

LYSISTRATA
                    All right, then.
I'll stay here to help you play with him.
We'll warm him up together. You others,   990
go inside.

[The women go inside, including Myrrhine. Lysistrata remains on stage. Cinesias enters with a very large erection. An attendant comes with him carrying a young baby]

CINESIAS
                    I'm in a dreadful way.
It's all this throbbing. And the strain. I feel
as if I'm stretched out on the rack.

LYSISTRATA
                    Who's there,
standing inside our line of sentinels?

CINESIAS
It's me.

LYSISTRATA
        A man?

CINESIAS *[waving his erection]*
                    Yes, take a look at this!

LYSISTRATA
In that case leave. Go on your way.

CINESIAS
                    Who are you
to tell me to get out?

LYSISTRATA
                    The daytime watch.

CINESIAS
Then, by the gods, call Myrrhine for me.   [850]

53

LYSISTRATA

You tell me to summon Myrrhine for you?
Who are you?

CINESIAS

             Cinesias, her husband,   1000
from Paeonidae.[1]

LYSISTRATA

             Welcome, dear friend, your name
is not unknown to us. Your wife always
has you on her lips. Any time she licks
an apple or an egg she says, "Ah me,
if only this could be Cinesias."

[Lysistrata licks her fist obscenely]

CINESIAS

             O my god!

LYSISTRATA

Yes, by Aphrodite, yes. And when our talk
happens to deal with men, your wife speaks up
immediately, "O they're all useless sorts   [860]
compared to my Cinesias."

CINESIAS

             Please call her out.

LYSISTRATA

Why should I do that? What will you give me?   1010

CINESIAS

Whatever you want, by god. I have this . . .

[Cinesias waves his erection in front of Lysistrata]

I'll give you what I've got.

LYSISTRATA

             No thanks.
I think I'll tell her to come out to you.

---

[1] *Paeonidae.* Sommerstein (p. 200) points out that Paeonidae is a political district in northern Attica. The name suggests the Greek verb *paiein,* meaning to strike or copulate. Sommerstein offers the translation "Bangwell." Jack Lindsay translates the place as "Bangtown."

[Lysistrata leaves to fetch Myrrhine]

CINESIAS
Hurry up. I've had no pleasure in life
since she's been gone from home. I go out,
but I'm in pain. To me now everything
seems empty. There's no joy in eating food.
I'm just so horny.

[Lysistrata appears dragging Myrrhine with her. Myrrhine is pretending to be reluctant]

MYRRHINE *[loudly so that Cinesias can hear]*
                    I love him. I do.
But he's unwilling to make love to me,   [870]
to love me back. Don't make me go to him.   1020

CINESIAS
O my dear sweetest little Myrrhine,
what are you doing? Come down here.

MYRRHINE
I'm not going there, by god.

CINESIAS
            If I ask you,
won't you come down, Myrrhine?

MYRRHINE
You've got no reason to be calling me.
You don't want me.

CINESIAS
            You don't think I want you?
I'm absolutely dying for you!

MYRRHINE
            I'm leaving.

CINESIAS
Hold on! You might want to hear our child.
Can you call out something to your mama?

CHILD
Mummy, mummy, mummy!

CINESIAS

What's wrong with you?   1030   [880]
Don't you feel sorry for the boy? It's now
six days since he's been washed or had some food.

MYRRHINE

Ah yes, I pity him. But it's quite clear
his father doesn't.

CINESIAS

My lovely wife,
come down here to the child.

MYRRHINE

Being a mother
is so demanding. I better go down.
What I put with!

*[Myrrhine starts coming down from the Acropolis accentuating the
movement of her hips as she goes]*

CINESIAS

She seems to me
to be much younger, easier on the eyes.
She was acting like a shrew and haughty,
but that just roused my passion even more.   1040

MYRRHINE *[to the child]*

My dear sweet little boy. But your father—
such a rotten one. Come here. I'll hold you.   [890]
Mummy's little favourite.

CINESIAS

You dim-witted girl,
what are you doing, letting yourself
be led on by these other women,
causing me grief and injuring yourself?

MYRRHINE

Don't lay a hand on me!

CINESIAS

Inside our home
things are a mess. You stopped doing anything.

56

MYRRHINE
I don't care.

CINESIAS
You don't care your weaving
is being picked apart by hens?

MYRRHINE
So what?   1050

CINESIAS
You haven't honoured holy Aphrodite
by having sex, not for a long time now.
So won't you come back?

MYRRHINE
No, by god, I won't—   [900]
unless you give me something in return.
End this war.

CINESIAS
Well now, that's something I'll do,
when the time seems right.

MYRRHINE
Well then, I'll leave here,
when the time seems right. But now I'm under oath.

CINESIAS
At least lie down with me a little while.

MYRRHINE
I can't. I'm not saying I wouldn't like to.

CINESIAS
You'd like to? Then, my little Myrrhine,   1060
lie down right here.

MYRRHINE
You must be joking—
in front of our dear baby child?

CINESIAS
No, by god!

[Cinesias turns toward the attendant]

57

Manes, take the boy back home. All right then,
the lad's no longer in the way. Lie down.

MYRRHINE
But, you silly man, where do we do it? [910]

CINESIAS
Where? The Cave of Pan's an excellent place.

MYRRHINE
How will I purify myself when I return
into the citadel?

CINESIAS
                                    You can wash yourself
in the water clock. That would do the job.

MYRRHINE
What about the oath I swore? Should I become   1070
a wretched perjurer?

CINESIAS
                                    I'll deal with that.
Don't worry about the oath.

MYRRHINE
                                    Well then,
I'll go and get a bed for us.

CINESIAS
                                    No, no.
The ground will do.

MYRRHINE
                                    No, by Apollo, no!
You may be a rascal, but on the ground?
No, I won't make you lie down there.

[Myrrhine goes back into the Acropolis to fetch a bed]

CINESIAS
                                    Ah, my wife—
she really loves me. That's so obvious.

[Myrrhine reappears carrying a small bed]

58

MYRRHINE
Here we are. Get on there while I undress.   [920]
O dear! I forgot to bring the mattress.

CINESIAS
Why a mattress? I don't need that.

MYRRHINE
                                        You can't lie   1080
on the bed cord. No, no, by Artemis,
that would be a great disgrace.

CINESIAS
                            Give me a kiss—
right now!

MYRRHINE [kissing him]
                            There you go.

[Myrrhine goes back to the Acropolis to fetch the mattress]

CINESIAS
                            Oh my god—
get back here quickly!

[Myrrhine reappears with the mattress]

MYRRHINE
                            Here's the mattress.
You lie down on it. I'll get my clothes off.
O dear me! You don't have a pillow.

CINESIAS
But I don't need a pillow!

MYRRHINE
                            By god, I do.

[Myrrhine goes back to the Acropolis for a pillow]

CINESIAS
This cock of mine is just like Hercules—   ]
he's being denied his supper.[1]

[Myrrhine returns with a pillow]

[1]Hercules was famous for always being hungry and having an enormous appetite.

MYRRHINE

Lift up a bit.
Come on, up! There, I think that's everything. 1090

CINESIAS
That's all we need. Come here, my treasure. [930]

MYRRHINE
I'm taking off the cloth around my breasts.
Now, don't forget. Don't you go lying to me
about that vote for peace.

CINESIAS

O my god,
may I die before that happens!

MYRRHINE

There's no blanket.

CINESIAS
I don't need one, by god! I want to get laid!

MYRRHINE
Don't worry. You will be. I'll be right back.

[Myrrhine goes back to the Acropolis to fetch a blanket]

CINESIAS
That woman's killing me with all the bedding!

[Myrrhine returns with a blanket]

MYRRHINE
All right, get up.

CINESIAS

But it's already up!

MYRRHINE
You want me to rub some scent on you? 1100

CINESIAS
No, by Apollo. Not for me.

MYRRHINE

I'll do it,
whether you want it rubbed on there or not—

60

for Aphrodite's sake.

[Myrrhine goes back to the Acropolis to get the perfume]

CINESIAS

O great lord Zeus,   [940]
pour the perfume out!

[Myrrhine returns with the perfume]

MYRRHINE

Hold out your hand, now.
Take that and spread it round.

CINESIAS *[rubbing the perfume on himself]*

By Apollo,
this stuff doesn't smell so sweet, not unless
it's rubbed on thoroughly—no sexy smell.

MYRRHINE *[inspecting the jar of perfume]*
I'm such a fool. I brought the Rhodian scent!

CINESIAS
It's fine. Just let it go, my darling.

MYRRHINE *[getting up to leave]*
You're just saying that.

[Myrrhine goes back to the Acropolis to get the right perfume]

CINESIAS
Damn the wretch who first came up with perfume!   1110

*[Myrrhine comes back from the Acropolis with another box of perfume
and takes off the top]*

MYRRHINE
Grab this alabaster thing.

CINESIAS *[waving his phallus]*
You grab this alabaster cock.
Come lie down here, you tease. Don't go and fetch
another thing for me.

MYRRHINE
By Artemis, I'll grab it.
I'm taking off my shoes. Now, my darling,   [950]

61

you will be voting to bring on a peace.

CINESIAS
I'm planning to.

[Myrrhine goes back to the Acropolis. Cinesias turns and sees she's gone]

                               That woman's killing me!
She teased me, got me all inflamed, then left.

[Cinesias gets up and declaims in a parody of tragic style]

Alas, why suffer from such agony?
Who can I screw? Why'd she betray me,
the most beautiful woman of them all?   1120
Poor little penis, how can I care for you?
Where's that Cynalopex? I'll pay him well
to nurse this little fellow back to health.[1]

LEADER OF MEN'S CHORUS
You poor man, in such a fix—your spirit
so tricked and in distress. I pity you.   [960]
How can your kidneys stand the strain,
your balls, your loins, your bum, your brain
endure an erection, so hard on you
without a chance of a morning screw.

CINESIAS
O mighty Zeus, it's started throbbing once again!   1130

LEADER OF MEN'S CHORUS
A dirty stinking bitch did this to you.

CINESIAS
No, by god, a loving girl, a sweet one, too.   [970]

LEADER OF MEN'S CHORUS
Sweet? Not her. She's a tease, a slut.

CINESIAS
All right, she is a tease, but—
O Zeus, Zeus, I wish
you'd sweep her up there

---

[1] *Cynalopex* (= "Fox Dog") was the nickname of Philostratus who apparently was a pimp.

in a great driving storm,
like dust in the air,
whirl her around,
then fall to the ground.   1140
Then as she's carried down,
to earth one more time,
let her fall right away
on this stiff prick of mine.

*[Enter the Spartan herald. He, too, has a giant erection, which he is
trying to hide under his cloak]*

SPARTAN HERALD
Where's the Athenian Senate and the Prytanes?[1]   [980]
I come with fresh dispatches.

CINESIAS [2]*[looking at the Herald's erection]*
                              Are you a man,
or some phallic monster?

SPARTAN HERALD
                              I'm a herald,
by the twin gods. And my good man,
I come from Sparta with a proposal,
arrangements for a truce.

CINESIAS
                              If that's the case,   1150
why do you have a spear concealed in there?

SPARTAN HERALD
I'm not concealing anything, by god.

CINESIAS
Then why are you turning to one side?
What that thing there, sticking from your cloak?
Has your trip given you a swollen groin?

---

[1] *Prytanes* was the business committee of the Athenian council.

[2] Some editors and translators assign Cinesias' role in this scene to the Magistrate, since
we have no reason to assume that Cinesias is a public official who would deal with a
diplomatic envoy from another state.

SPARTAN HERALD
By old Castor, this man's insane!

CINESIAS
You rogue,
you've got a hard on!

SPARTAN HERALD
No I don't, I tell you.   [990]
Let's have no more nonsense.

CINESIAS *[pointing to the herald's erection]*
Then what's that?

SPARTAN HERALD
It's a Spartan herald's stick.

CINESIAS
O that's what it is,
a Spartan herald stick. Let's have a chat.   1160
Tell me the truth. How are things going for you
out there in Sparta?

SPARTAN HERALD
Not good. The Spartans
are all standing tall and the allies, too—
everyone is firm and hard. We need a thrust
in someone's rear.[1]

CINESIAS
This trouble of yours—
where did it come from? Was it from Pan?[2]

SPARTAN HERALD
No. I think it started with Lampito.
Then, at her suggestion, other women
in Sparta, as if from one starting gate,
ran off to keep men from their honey pots.   1170   [1000]

---

[1] ... *in someone's rear.* The Greek reads "we need Pellene," an area in the Peloponnese allied with Sparta. But, as Sommerstein points out (p. 206), this is undoubtedly a pun invoking a word meaning vagina or anus. In the exchanges which follow, the Spartans are depicted as having a decided preference for anal sex.

[2] *Pan* was a god associated with wild unrestrained sex in the wilderness .

CINESIAS
How are you doing?

SPARTAN HERALD
We're all in pain.
We go around the city doubled up,
like men who light the lamps.[1] The women
won't let us touch their pussies, not until
we've made a peace with all of Greece.

CINESIAS
This matter
is a female plot, a grand conspiracy
affecting all of Greece. Now I understand.
Return to Sparta as fast as you can go.
Tell them they must send out ambassadors   [1010]
with full authority to deal for peace.   1180
I'll tell out leaders here to make a choice
of our ambassadors. I'll show them my prick.

SPARTAN HERALD
All you've said is good advice. I must fly.

[Cinesias and the Spartan Herald exit in opposite directions]

LEADER OF MEN'S CHORUS
There's no wild animal harder to control
than women, not even blazing fire.
The panther itself displays more shame.

LEADER OF WOMEN'S CHORUS
If you know that, then why wage war with me?
You old scoundrel, we could be lasting friends.

LEADER OF MEN'S CHORUS
But my hatred for women will not stop!

LEADER OF WOMEN'S CHORUS
Whatever you want. But I don't much like   1190
to look at you like this, without your clothes.   [1020]
It makes me realize how silly you are.
Look, I'll come over and put your tunic on.

---

[1] *men who light the lamps.* The lamplighters had to walk along bent over in order to
protect the flame they carried.

*[The Leader of the Women's Chorus picks up a tunic, goes over to the
Leader of the Men's Chorus, and helps him put it on.]*

LEADER OF MEN'S CHORUS
By god, what you've just done is not so bad.
I took it off in a fit of stupid rage.

LEADER OF WOMEN'S CHORUS
Now at least you look like a man again.
And people won't find you ridiculous.
If you hadn't been so nasty to me,
I'd grab that insect stuck inside your eye
and pull it out. It's still in there.   1200

LEADER OF MEN'S CHORUS
So that's what's been troubling me. Here's a ring.
Scrape it off. Get it out and show it to me.
God, that's been injuring my eye for ages.

*[The Leader of the Women's Chorus takes the ring and inspects the
Leader of the Men's Chorus in the eye]*

LEADER OF WOMEN'S CHORUS
I'll do it. You men are born hard to please.   [1030]
My god, you picked up a monstrous insect.
Have a look. That's a Tricorynthus bug![1]

LEADER OF MEN'S CHORUS
By Zeus, you've been a mighty help to me.
That thing's been digging wells in me a while.
Now it's been removed, my eyes are streaming.

LEADER OF WOMEN'S CHORUS
I'll wipe it for you, though you're a scoundrel.   1210
I'll give you a kiss.

LEADER OF THE MEN'S CHORUS
                              I don't want a kiss.

LEADER OF WOMEN'S CHORUS
I will, whether it's what you want or not.

[She kisses him]

---

[1] *Tricorynthus* is a region in Attica, near Marathon. Presumably it was famous for its
insects.

LEADER OF MEN'S CHORUS
O you've got me. You're born to flatter us.
That saying got it right—it states the case
quite well, "These women—one has no life ⌉
with them and cannot live without them." ⌡
But now I'll make a truce with you. I won't   [1040]
insult you any more in days to come,
and you won't make me suffer. So now,
let's make a common group and sing a song.   1220

[The Men's and Women's Choruses combine]

COMBINED CHORUS *[addressing the audience]*
You citizens, we're not inclined
with any of you to be unkind.
Just the reverse—our words to you
will be quite nice. We'll act well, too.
For now we've had enough bad news.
So if a man or woman here   [1050]
needs ready cash, give out a cheer,
and take some minae, two or three.
Coins fill our purses now, you see.
And if we get a peace treaty,   1230
you take some money from the sack,
and keep it. You don't pay it back.
I'm going to have a great shindig—
I've got some soup, I'll kill a pig—
with Carystian friends, all good men.[1]   [1060]
You'll eat fine tender meat again.
Come to my house this very day.
But first wash all the dirt away,
you and your kids, then walk on by.
No need to ask a person why.   1240
Just come straight in, as if my home
was like your own—for at my place   [1070]
we'll shut the door right in your face.

[A group of Spartans enters]

LEADER OF THE CHORUS
Ah, here come the Spartan ambassadors

---

[1] *Carystus* is a state from Euboea, allied to Athens.

trailing their long beards. They've got
something like pig sticks between their thighs.

*[The Spartan ambassadors enter, moving with difficulty because of
their enormous erections.]*

Men of Sparta, first of all, our greetings.
Tell us how you are. Why have you come?

SPARTAN AMBASSADOR
Why waste a lot of words to tell you?
You see the state that brought us here.   1250

[The Spartans all display their erections with military precision]

LEADER OF THE CHORUS
Oh my! The crisis has grown more severe.
It seems the strain is worse than ever.

SPARTAN AMBASSADOR
It's indescribable. What can I say?   [1080]
But let someone come, give us a peace
in any way he can.

[The Athenian ambassadors enter, also moving with difficulty]

LEADER OF THE CHORUS
                Well now, I see
our own ambassadors—they look just like
our wrestling men with their shirts sticking out
around their bellies or like athletic types
who need to exercise to cure their sickness.

ATHENIAN AMBASSADOR
Where's Lysistrata? Can someone tell me?   1260
We're men here and, well, look . . .

*[The Athenians pull back their cloaks and reveal that, like the Spartans,
they all have giant erections]*

LEADER OF THE CHORUS
They're clearly suffering from the same disease.
Hey, does it throb early in the morning?

ATHENIAN AMBASSADOR
By god, yes. What this is doing to me—   [1090]

68

it's torture. If we don't get a treaty soon
we'll going to have to cornhole Cleisthenes.[1] —

LEADER OF THE CHORUS

If you're smart, keep it covered with your cloak.
One of those men who chopped off Hermes' dick
might see you.[2]

ATHENIAN AMBASSADOR

By god, that's good advice.   1270

SPARTAN AMBASSADOR

Yes, by the twin gods, you counsel well.
I'll pull my mantle over it.

ATHENIAN AMBASSADOR

Greetings, Spartans.
We're both suffering disgracefully.

SPARTAN AMBASSADOR

Yes, dear sir, we'd have been in real pain
if one of those dick-clippers had seen us
with our peckers sticking up like this.

ATHENIAN AMBASSADOR

All right, Spartans, we each need to talk.   [1100]
Why are you here?

SPARTAN AMBASSADOR

Ambassadors for peace.

ATHENIAN AMBASSADOR

Well said. We want the same. Why don't we call
Lysistrata. She's the only one who'll bring   1280
a resolution to our differences.

SPARTAN AMBASSADOR

By the two gods, bring in Lysistratus,
if he's the one you want.

[Lysistrata emerges from the gates of the citadel]

---

[1] *Cleisthenes*: a well known Athenian, whom Aristophanes frequently ridicules as a
passive homosexual.

[2] *Hermes' dick*: In 415 the statues of Hermes in Athens were mutilated by having their
penises chopped off, a very sacrilegious act .

ATHENIAN AMBASSADOR
It seems there is no need to summon her.
She's heard us, and here she is in person.

LEADER OF THE CHORUS
Hail to the bravest woman of them all.
You must now show that you're resilient—
stern but yielding, with a good heart but mean,
stately but down-to-earth. The foremost men
in all of Greece in deference to your charms   1290   [1110]
have come together here before you
so you can arbitrate all their complaints.

LYSISTRATA
That task should not be difficult, unless
they're so aroused they hump each other.
I'll quickly notice that. But where is she,
the young girl Reconciliation?

*[The personification of the goddess Reconciliation comes out. She is
completely naked. Lysistrata addresses her first]*[1]

Come here,
and first, take hold of those from Sparta,
don't grab too hard or be too rough, not like
our men who act so boorishly—instead
do it as women do when they're at home.   1300
⌈ If they won't hold out their hands to you,
⌊ then grab their penises.

*[Reconciliation takes two Spartans by their penises and leads them over
to Lysistrata]*

Now go and do the same   [1120]
for the Athenians. You can hold them
by whatever they stick out.

[Reconciliation leads the Athenians over to Lysistrata]

Now then,
you men of Sparta, stand here close to me,

---

[1]*Reconciliation:* In Aristophanes' time, this character would be played by a man with
a body stocking prominently displaying female characteristics: breasts, pubic hair,
buttocks.

70

and you Athenians over here. All of you,
listen to my words. I am a woman,
but I have a brain, and my common sense
is not so bad—I picked it up quite well
from listening to my father and to speeches   1310
from our senior men. Now I've got you here,
I wish to reprimand you, both of you,
and rightly so. At Olympia, Delphi,   [1130]
and Thermopylae (and I could mention
many other places if I had a mind
to make it a long list) both of you
use the same cup when you sprinkle altars,
as if you share the same ancestral group.[1]
We've got barbarian enemies, and yet
with your armed expeditions you destroy   1320
Greek men and cities. At this point, I'll end
the first part of my speech.

ATHENIAN AMBASSADOR
                    This erection—
it's killing me!

LYSISTRATA
                    And now you Spartans,
I'll turn to you. Don't you remember how,
some time ago, Periclidias came,
a fellow Spartan, and sat down right here,
a suppliant at these Athenian altars—   [1140]
he looked so pale there in his purple robes—
begging for an army? Messenians then
were pressing you so hard, just at the time   1330
god sent the earthquake. So Cimon set off
with four thousand armed infantry and saved
the whole of Sparta.[2] After going through that,
how can you lay waste the Athenians' land,

---

[1] *Olympia, Delphi, Thermopylae.* Lysistrata is listing some of the festivals where all the
Greek states cooperated in the ritual celebrations.

[2] *. . . the whole of Sparta.* In 464 BC Sparta suffered a massive earthquake, which killed
many citizens. Their slaves, who included the Messenians, rose in revolt. Sparta
appealed to Athens for help, and the Athenians, after some debate, sent Cimon with an
army to assist the Spartans.

the ones who helped you out?

ATHENIAN AMBASSADOR
                                    Lysistrata,
you're right, by god. They're in the wrong.

SPARTAN AMBASSADOR *[looking at Reconciliation]*
                                    Not true,
but look at that incredibly fine ass!

LYSISTRATA
Do you Athenians think I'll forget you?
Don't you remember how these Spartan men,   [1150]
back in the days when you were dressed as slaves   1340
came here with spears and totally destroyed
those hordes from Thessaly and many friends
of Hippias and those allied with him?
It took them just one day to drive them out
and set you free. At that point you exchanged
your slavish clothes for cloaks which free men wear.[1]

SPARTAN AMBASSADOR
I've never seen a more gracious woman.

ATHENIAN AMBASSADOR *[looking at Reconciliation]*
I've never seen a finer looking pussy.

LYSISTRATA
If you've done many good things for each other,
why go to war? Why not stop this conflict?   1350   [1160]
Why not conclude a peace? What's in the way?

[In the negotiations which follow, the ambassadors use the body of Reconciliation as a map of Greece, pointing to various parts to make their points]

SPARTAN AMBASSADOR
We're willing, but the part that's sticking out
we want that handed back.

LYSISTRATA
                          Which one is that?

---

[1]In 510 the Spartans helped the Athenians overthrow the last of the tyrants, Hippias.

SPARTAN AMBASSADOR *[pointing to Reconciliation's buttocks]*
This one here—that's Pylos. We must have that—
we've been aching for it a long time now.[1]

ATHENIAN AMBASSADOR
By Poseidon, you won't be having that!

LYSISTRATA
My good man, you'll surrender it to them.

ATHENIAN AMBASSADOR
Then how do we make trouble, stir up shit?

LYSISTRATA
Ask for something else of equal value.

ATHENIAN AMBASSADOR *[inspecting Reconciliation's body and
pointing to her public hair]*
Then give us this whole area in here—   1360
first, there's Echinous, and the Melian Gulf,
the hollow part behind it, and these legs   [1170]
which make up Megara.[2]

SPARTAN AMBASSADOR
                              By the twin gods,
my good man, you can't have all that!

LYSISTRATA
                              Let it go.
Don't start fighting over a pair of legs.

ATHENIAN AMBASSADOR
I'd like to strip and start ploughing naked.

SPARTAN AMBASSADOR
By god, yes! But me first. I'll fork out manure.

LYSISTRATA
You can do those things once you've made peace.
If these terms seem good, you'll want your allies
to come here to join negotiations.   1370

---

[1]Pylos was a small but important part of the south Peloponnese which the Athenians
had seized in 425 and held onto ever since.

[2]*Echinous . . . Melian Gulf . . . Megara*: These are places relatively close to Athens.

73

ATHENIAN AMBASSADORS
What of our allies? We've all got hard ons.
Our allies will agree this is just fine.
They're all dying to get laid!

SPARTAN AMBASSADOR
                              Ours, as well—   [1180]
no doubt of that.

ATHENIAN AMBASSADOR
                    And the Carystians—
they'll also be on board, by Zeus.

LYSISTRATA
Well said. Now you must purify yourselves.
We women will host a dinner for you
in the Acropolis. We'll use the food
we brought here in our baskets. In there
you will make a oath and pledge your trust   1380
in one another. Then each of you
can take his wife and go back home.

ATHENIAN AMBASSADOR
                              Let's go—
and hurry up.

SPARTAN AMBASSADOR [to Lysistrata]
                    Lead on. Wherever you wish.

ATHENIAN AMBASSADOR
All right by Zeus, as fast as we can go.

[Lysistrata and Reconciliation lead the Spartan and Athenian delega-
tions into the Acropolis]

CHORUS
Embroidered gowns and shawls,
robes and golden ornaments—
everything I own—I offer you
with an open heart. Take these things
and let your children have them,
if you've a daughter who will be   1390
a basket bearer. I tell you all
take my possessions in my home—

74

nothing is so securely closed
you can't break open all the seals
and take whatever's there inside.   [1200]
But if you look, you won't see much
unless your eyesight's really keen,
far more perceptive than my own.
If anyone is out of corn
to feed his many tiny children   1400
and household slaves, at home
I've got a few fine grains of wheat—
a quart of those will make some bread,
a fresh good-looking loaf. If there's a man
who wants some bread and is in need   [1210]
let him come with his sacks and bags
to where I live to get his wheat.
My servant Manes will pour it out.
But I should tell you not to come
too near my door—there is a dog   1410
you need to stay well clear of.

ATHENIAN DELEGATE A *[from inside the citadel]*
          Open the door!

*[The Athenian Delegate A comes staggering out of the citadel, evi-
dently drunk. He's carrying a torch. Other delegates in the same
condition come out behind him. Athenian Delegate A bumps into one
of a group of Spartan slaves standing around waiting for their masters
to come out]*[1]

ATHENIAN DELEGATE A
                    Why don't you get out of my way?
          Why are you lot sitting there? What if I
          burned you with this torch? That's a stale routine![2]

----

[1] *. . . by the door.* The stage business at this point is somewhat confusing. It's not clear
whether the Athenian delegates who now appear are leaving the meeting in the citadel
or arriving and wanting to get in. Here I follow Sommerstein, who is following
Henderson, and have the delegates emerge from the meeting. The people hanging
around the door are probably the slaves who came with the Spartans and who are
waiting for their masters inside.

[2] *. . . stale routine.* This comment is mocking other comic dramatists who use a stock set
of situations or actions, while at the same time the action uses the stock technique (not
an uncommon feature of Aristophanic comedy).

I won't do that. Well, if I really must,
to keep you happy, I'll go through with it. [1220]

[Athenian Delegate A chases an onlooker away with his torch]

ATHENIAN DELEGATE B *[waving a torch]*
We'll be here with you to help you do it.
Why not just leave? You may soon be screaming
for that hair of yours.

ATHENIAN DELEGATE A
                              Go on, piss off!
So the Spartans inside there can come on out   1420
and go away in peace.

*[The two Athenian delegates force the Spartan slaves away from the
door]*

ATHENIAN DELEGATE B
                              Well now,
I never seen a banquet quite like this.
The Spartans were delightful. As for us,
we had too much wine, but as companions
we said lots of really clever things.

ATHENIAN DELEGATE A
That's right. When we're sober, we lose our minds.
I'll speak up and persuade Athenians
that when our embassies go anywhere   [1230]
they stay permanently drunk. As it is,
whenever we go sober off to Sparta,   1430
right away we look to stir up trouble.
So we just don't hear what they have to say
and get suspicious of what they don't state.
Then we bring back quite different reports
about the same events. But now these things
have all been sorted out. So if someone there
sang "Telamon" when he should have sung
"Cleitagora," we'd applaud the man
and even swear quite falsely that . . .[1]

[The Spartan slaves they forced away from the door come back]

[1]"Telamon" and "Cleitagora" are well known drinking songs.

76

                          Hey, those slaves
are coming here again. You whipping posts,   1440   [1240]
why can't you go away?

ATHENIAN DELEGATE B
                          By Zeus,
the ones in there are coming out again.

[The Spartan delegates come out of the citadel. The Spartan ambas-
sador is carrying a musical instrument]

SPARTAN AMBASSADOR
Here, my dear sir, take this wind instrument,
so I can dance and sing a lovely song
to honour both Athenians and ourselves.

ATHENIAN AMBASSADOR *[turning to one of the slaves]*
Yes, by the gods, take the pipes. I love
to see you Spartans dance and sing.

[The music starts. The Spartan Ambassador sings and dances]

SPARTAN AMBASSADOR
O Memory, to this young man
send down your child the Muse
who knows the Spartans and Athenians.[1]   1450   [1250]
Back then at Artemesium
they fought the ships like gods of war
and overpowered the Medes,
while we, I know, led by Leonidas
whetted our gnashing teeth like boars,
mouths full of foam—it dripped
down on our legs. The Persian force
possessed more fighting men
than grains of sea shore sand.   [1260]
O Artemis, queen of the wild,   1460
slayer of beasts, chaste goddess,
come here to bless our treaty,
to make us long united.
May our peace be always blessed

---

[1]The Spartan Ambassador is singing about two famous battles against the Persians (both
in 480), the Athenian naval victory at Artemisium and the Spartan stand of the 300 at
Thermopylae. These military campaigns were important highlights of Greek unity.

77

with friendship and prosperity,
and may we put an end
to all manipulating foxes.   [1270]
Come here, O come here,
Virgin Goddess of the Hunt.

[Lysistrata emerges from the citadel bringing all the wives with her]

LYSISTRATA[1]
Come now, since everything has turned out well,   1470
take these women back with you, you Spartans.
And, you Athenians, these ones are yours.
Let each man stand beside his wife, each wife
beside her man, and then to celebrate
good times let's dance in honour of the gods.
And for all future time, let's never make
the same mistake again.

[The Chorus now sings to the assembled group, as the wives and husbands are rejoined]

CHORUS
Lead on the dance, bring on the Graces,
and summon Artemis and her twin,   [1280]
Apollo, the god who heals us all.   1480
Call on Bacchus, Nysa's god,
whose eyes blaze forth
amid his Maenads' ecstasy,
and Zeus alight with flaming fire,
and Hera, Zeus' blessed wife,
and other gods whom we will use
as witnesses who won't forget
the meaning of the gentle Peace
made here by goddess Aphrodite.   [1290]
Alalai! Raise the cry of joy,   1490
raise it high, iai!
the cry of victory, iai!
Evoi, evoi, evoi, evoi!

LYSISTRATA
Spartan, now offer us another song,

[1]There is some dispute about the character to whom this speech should be assigned.
Sommerstein (p. 221) has a useful summary of the arguments.

match our new song with something new.

SPARTAN AMBASSADOR
Leave lovely Taygetus once more
and, Spartan Muse, in some way
that is appropriate for us
pay tribute to Amyclae's god,
and to bronze-housed Athena,   1500
to Tyndareus' splendid sons,   [1300]
who play beside the Eurotas.
Step now, with many a nimble turn,
so we may sing a hymn to Sparta,
dancing in honour of the gods,
with stamping feet in that place
where by the river Eurotas
young maidens dance,
like fillies raising dust,   [1310]
tossing their manes,   1510
like those bacchants, who play
and wave their thyrsus stalks,
led on by Leda's lovely child,
their holy leader in the choral dance.[1]
But come, let your hands bind up your hair.
Let your feet leap up like deer,
sound out the beat to help our dance.
Let a song of praise ring out
for our mighty bronze-house goddess,
all-conquering Athena!   1520

[They all exit singing and dancing]

---

[1] *Taygetus* is an important mountain in Sparta. *Amyclae's god* is Apollo who had a shrine at Amyclae, near Sparta. *Bronze-housed Athena* is a reference to the shrine of Athena in Sparta. *Tyndareus' splendid sons* are Castor and Pollux, the twin gods (brothers of Helen and Clytaemnestra). The *Eurotas* is a river near Sparta. The *thyrsus stalk* is a plant stem held by the followers of Bacchus in their ecstatic dancing. *Leda's child* is Helen (wife of Menelaus, sister of Castor and Pollux and Clytaemnestra, a child of Zeus).

A NOTE ON THE TRANSLATOR

Ian Johnston is a retired university instructor, now an Emeritus Professor at Vancouver Island University, Nanaimo, British Columbia. He has translated a number of works, including the following:

Aeschylus, *Oresteia*
Aeschylus, *Persians*
Aeschylus, *Prometheus Bound*
Aeschylus, *Seven Against Thebes*
Aeschylus, *Suppliant Women*
Aristophanes, *Birds*
Aristophanes, *Clouds*
Aristophanes, *Frogs*
Aristophanes, *Knights*
Aristophanes, *Lysistrata*
Aristophanes, *Peace*
Cuvier, *Discourse on Revolutionary Upheavals on the Surface of the Earth*
Descartes, *Discourse on Method*
Descartes, *Meditations*
Diderot, D'Alembert's Dream and Rameau's Nephew
Euripides, *Bacchae*
Euripides, *Medea*
Euripides, *Orestes*
Homer, *Iliad* (Complete and Abridged)
Homer, *Odyssey* (Complete and Abridged)
Kant, *Universal Natural History and Theory of the Heavens*
Kant, *On Perpetual Peace*
Lucretius, *The Nature of Things*
Nietzsche, *Beyond Good and Evil*
Nietzsche, *Birth of Tragedy*
Nietzsche, *Genealogy of Morals*
Nietzsche, *Uses and Abuses of History*
Ovid, *Metamorphoses*
Rousseau, *The First and Second Discourses*
Rousseau, *On the Social Contract or Principles of Political Right*
Sophocles, *Ajax*
Sophocles, *Antigone*
Sophocles, *Oedipus the King*
Sophocles, *Philoctetes*

A number of these translations have been published by Richer Resources Publications, and some of these titles are available as recordings from Naxos Audiobooks.

Ian Johnston maintains a website at the following address:
records.viu.ca/~johnstoi/index.htm.

For comments and questions, please contact Ian Johnston (at ian.johnston@viu.ca).